HUGH GREEN'S STIRLINGSHIRE

HUGH GREEN (1892 - 1973)

• • •

James Wedlake

Published in 2014 by the Stirling Smith Art Gallery and Museum
Text copyright © James Wedlake
Illustrations copyright © Stirling Smith Art Gallery and Museum unless otherwise stated
Design by Heather Ann Dowd Ltd

ISBN 0-9546511-8-9

Printed by S & G Print Group
Front cover: Stirling from the Raploch, body colour on paper, 1972, 320 x 485, collection of the Stirling Smith.

THE EXHIBITION AND PUBLICATION Hugh Green's Stirlingshire was curated and researched by Museums Galleries Scotland Intern James Wedlake, working at the Stirling Smith Art Gallery and Museum in 2014. Work included sourcing the exhibits, negotiating loans, conducting interviews, photography, digitisation of images, writing and designing publicity material, selecting frames, gallery preparation and exhibition presentation. This was done in addition to an intensive year long programme of training and work experience.

James Wedlake made full use of the opportunity to record the details of Green's life and work through interviewing relatives and people who knew him. In some respects Green was not a typical house painter. Many of his contemporaries contracted chest complaints and died in their forties, like Robert Noonan (1870 - 1911), who under the pen name of Robert Tressell wrote *The Ragged Trousered Philanthropists*. The novel is a searing account of working conditions and practices in the trades of house painting and sign writing. First published in 1914, and scarcely out of print since, it quickly became "the Painter's Bible", given to every apprentice who entered the trade.

Green lived to the age of eighty, and was both able to make a living and pursue his art. Bridge of Allan was very different from Noonan's Hastings, but the circumstances were similar in that both Noonan's biographer and James Wedlake have had to dig deep to ascertain the facts and tell their respective stories. James has been able to contextualise Green's life and work as part of the rich and largely overlooked Arts & Crafts movement in Stirlingshire. Histories of artist - house decorators are few and far between and we are very proud of what James has achieved and gifted to Stirlingshire in his short time at the Smith, and are grateful to Museums Galleries Scotland for making it possible.

Elspeth King
Director
Stirling Smith Art Gallery and Museum

ACKNOWLEDGEMENTS

THE HUGH GREEN EXHIBITION has been made possible through the sponsorship of Craig & Rose Ltd, Bonhams: Scotland's International Saleroom and Norbord as well as through grant funding provided by Museums Galleries Scotland. The Stirling Smith would also like to thank all those who have loaned works for the exhibition and all those who have carried out interviews for the purpose of researching the life of Hugh Green. The museum is very grateful to Malcolm Allan and Ursula Shone for donating paintings by Green to the collection. Finally thanks are extended to the Bridge of Allan Times, for publishing an article on Hugh Green, the Dr Welsh Educational and Historical Trust for loaning works, the Friends of the Smith, the Stirling Council Archives and many members and associates of the Stirling Art Club.

New Arts Sponsorship Grants Supported by the Scottish Government In conjunction with

FOREWORD

THE EXHIBITION at the Stirling Smith brings together the best works of the Bridge of Allan based artist and designer Hugh Green. It is the first major exhibition to be devoted to the artist since his death in 1973. I am delighted that Craig & Rose Ltd have been able to work with the Stirling Smith Art Gallery & Museum to give Hugh Green the attention he deserves. Craig & Rose Ltd have transformed the gallery space through a donation of paint. No doubt Hugh Green, who was an interior decorator by trade, would have shared our belief in the power of paint to bring beauty to any interior!

Stephen Percy-Robb
Managing Director, Craig & Rose Ltd

INTRODUCTION

Hugh Green's paintings were first brought to the attention of the Stirling Smith by the Bridge of Allan based historian, J. Malcolm Allan.

MALCOLM DONATED SEVERAL LANDSCAPES to the Stirling Smith in 2010. He knew Hugh as an elderly gentleman. Both were members of the congregation of St Saviour's Episcopal Church, Bridge of Allan. Malcolm quite rightly considered Green's work worthy of recognition by the local museum.

Hugh Green did not seek to make a name as an artist during his lifetime and his work is part of the unwritten art history of Stirlingshire. He worked as a painter and decorator in order to earn a living, whereas he painted pictures in his spare time as an end in itself. The majority of his artistic output consists of paintings of the local area (fig. 1). He was a prolific artist and produced a staggeringly large number of artworks. In his youth he studied design at the Glasgow School of Art (GSA) and there he produced a number of Arts and Crafts designs. His sound training at the GSA would have provided a firm foundation for working on decorative schemes in houses in Bridge of Allan.

1. Stirling Castle, body colour on board, 1971, 570 x 830, collection of Yvonne Syme.

LIFE AT ALLANBANK WITH THE GREENS

The story of Hugh Green's parents, Hugh and Jane (née Arnott), can only be sketched out in brief.

THEY MARRIED ON 15 NOVEMBER 1889 at Kilsyth. At the time Hugh was twenty-five and Jane was twenty. They were both from Stirling. Jane was a domestic servant and lived in Broad Street whilst Hugh was a soldier and was stationed in the Castle. According to a niece of the artist Hugh Green's mother 'adored boys', but 'had no time for girls'.

Hugh Green was born in Alloa on 5 February 1892. He was baptised the same month in St Mungo's Parish Church. He was the first of Hugh and Jane's many children. In total he had seven siblings. From eldest to youngest they were: Janet (b.1894), Willie (b.1896), Davie (b.1897), Jack (b.1903), May (b.1904), Ella (b.1906) and James (b.1909). Hugh and Jane also had two children, who died as infants: Jane Elizabeth Arnott Green (1899-1901) and Christina Ann Arnott Green (February-May 1913).

The Green family moved to Bridge of Allan from Alloa sometime before 1894. They eventually settled in Allanbank, Allanvale Road, which Hugh Green depicted many times in his paintings. In many of these pictures most of Allanbank is hidden behind a no longer extant building, which burnt down in 1938 (fig. 2). The building used to contain the Bridge of Allan telephone exchange, which was later relocated to Fountain Road. Little is known of Hugh's youth except that, apparently,

2. Allanbank, body colour on paper, 370 x 505, collection of Yvonne Syme.

3. Hugh Green in military uniform, collection of Yvonne Syme.

he was a sprinter and raced at local games.[1] His father died from vascular disease in February 1913 aged forty-eight. He had supported the family as a postman and his death left Hugh the family breadwinner. When

Hugh's brothers, Willie and Davie, went away to fight in the Great War, Hugh was required to remain at home to support the family. To help the war effort he served with the Local Volunteer Force (fig. 3).

Allanbank, which is still standing today, contained six separate tenement houses, two on each floor. The flats were entered from the rear through an external communal stairway. The Green family lived in one of the two small flats on the first floor. Janet, Davie, Jack, Ella and James all moved out of Allanbank as they grew up. Ella's son, Norman, spent lots of time in Allanbank when he was a young boy in the 1930s. Robert Graham, Norman's father, had died when he was seven years old and since Ella had to work, Hugh Green's mother offered to look after Norman in the day. Hugh, Willie, May and their mother all remained in Allanbank for the rest of their lives. Hugh looked after his mother until she died in August 1943. He outlived both Willie (who died in 1964) and May (who died in 1968). In his last years he lived on his own.

The Greens had gas lighting and cooked on an old black coal fire range. The kitchen overlooked the Allan Water. Hugh would later win a competition at the local art club with a pastel study of the range.[2] There was a little room on the other side of the house, which the Greens referred to as 'the parlour'. Hugh used to keep all his paintings there. At times he had so many pictures there that they were stacked ten deep on every wall and around the big table in the centre of the room. There was a clock on the chest in the parlour, which Hugh's brother Willie had won in a sports competition. There was no bath in the flat, only a toilet and a sink. Hugh made very few alterations to the property whilst he lived there so that towards the end of his life stepping into Allanbank was like travelling back to another era. The

fact that Hugh was still using gas in the 1970s meant that he did not suffer when power cuts were a common occurrence.[3]

Helen Orchard and her grandson, Eddie, who was born on 3 November 1927, lived in one of the two flats on the second floor of Allanbank.[4] In the early thirties when Eddie was growing up the Black family lived in the other flat on the first floor next door to the Greens. Like Hugh, Mr Black was a house painter. At that time the Richardson family lived in one of the flats on the ground floor. Bill Richardson ran a grocery shop there. Mr and Mrs Berry and their daughter May, who was a little older than Norman, lived in the other flat on the ground floor. Sometime later one of the ground floor premises contained a reading room for the employees of the Kierfield textile works, which was run by the wealthy Pullar family.

Eddie and Norman went to school and played together. Eddie sang in the choir at St Saviour's as a boy, even though he would much rather have been playing football. When Eddie was young he worked as a butcher at Turnbull's. The factory was based in Queen's Lane, just around the corner from Allanbank. The company produced sausages, bacon and ham and distributed them all around Scotland. After the Turnbull's factory closed Eddie got a job at the Cape Asbestos Company (now Cape plc.). Eddie later served in the army.

---

[1] 'Mr Hugh Green', obituary from unknown paper provided by Ian Anderson. Some of the information in the obituary is inaccurate so this fact may or may not be true.

[2] Minute of a Stirling Art Club Meeting, January 31, 1958. Stirling Art Club Minute Book 1928-1938. Stirling Art Club Archives. Victoria Square, Stirling.

[3] Whilst Edward Heath was prime minister (1970-4) the country continually suffered from power cuts. Dwindling coal stocks and industrial action had led to a shortage of electricity and the implementation of the 'Three-Day Week' policy. Commercial organisations were limited to using electricity on three consecutive days per week.

[4] Much of the information regarding Allanbank was kindly supplied by Molly Orchard (b.1932), the widow of Eddie, and a friend of Hugh Green.

BRIDGE OF ALLAN IN BRIEF

Bridge of Allan, three miles north of Stirling and two miles south of Dunblane, began as a small settlement around the crossing point on Allan Water where a bridge was built in 1520.

THE AREA WAS KNOWN FOR ITS COPPER MINES and textile production. Discovery of mineral water springs by Sir Robert Abercrombie in the 1820s led to its development as a fashionable spa town. The popularity of the resort was greatly boosted by the publication of *A Week at Bridge of Allan* (1853), written by the Reverend Dr Charles Rogers, who at the same time was running campaigns to secure 'The Valley', the rough area beside Stirling Castle as a new burial ground whose layout would also serve as a guide to the history of the reformed Church of Scotland, and to build a national monument in honour of Sir William Wallace.

Bridge of Allan was laid out in sweeping avenues, with large, speculatively built mansions surrounded by landscaped gardens which were rented to wealthy families coming on holiday or to 'take the waters' in this 'Queen of Scottish Spas'. The size and number of these high ceilinged buildings provided employment for interior decorators, and still do.

At the height of its popularity as a resort, Bridge of Allan had many public facilities, including the Macfarlane Museum, replaced in 1886 by the Museum Hall which served as a multi-purpose concert, dance hall and museum. The Bridge of Allan Highland Games, established in 1851, are still going strong today. The Scottish Lawn Tennis Championships took place in Bridge of Allan in 1908 and today, the University of Stirling, established in 1967, is a recognised centre of excellence for sport.

The Bridge of Allan Gazette recorded visitors to the town. Famous visitors included the Stevenson family, engineers and lighthouse builders, with a young Robert Louis Stevenson whose imagination was fired by the secret places of Bridge of Allan. Famous artists included the American landscape painter George Inness, who witnessed a beautiful sunset in Bridge of Allan, 3 August 1894 immediately before his death, and the composer Chopin who visited in 1848.

Bridge of Allan today has a population of 4930.

HUGH GREEN'S APPEARANCE AND CHARACTER

Thanks to photographic evidence only a few remarks are required on the subject of Hugh Green's appearance.

MANY HAVE COMMENTED ON THE DIMINUTIVE height of the members of the Green family and Hugh was no exception. Like his sister May he was also 'stick thin'. Hugh lived his life in a thoughtful way and always dressed in a neat and tidy manner. One of his friends said she imagined he would have worn a tie, even when he was working on painting and decorating jobs in local houses.

Whilst Hugh's appearance needs little explanation, his character deserves more words if only to emphasise how noble it was. Self-effacing is the adjective that probably best describes him. This character trait led him not only to never seek personal gain, but also to always look out for the needs of others. Hugh was a very devout Christian and he conducted his life with perfect humility and selflessness, just as the word of God advises:

'Do nothing from selfish ambition or conceit, but in humility count others more significant than yourselves. Let each of you look not only to his own interests, but also to the interests of others.'[5]

Hugh Green appears never to have been troubled by ordinary earthly desires. He lived an ascetic lifestyle: he never smoked or drank, never married and appears never to have had any relationships. It is unsurprising, given Hugh's lifestyle, that the rector of the church once said of him: 'I have never met anyone so like a saint.

4, Puerto Soller, watercolour on paper, 1957, 560 x 700, collection of George McArthur.

---

[5] Phil. 2:3-11 (ESV).

That man's a saint!' One relative said he was the only man he has ever met who was absolutely cut out to be a priest. However, he was always very quiet about his religious beliefs and did not preach to others.

Hugh never looked for people's attention and never pursued glory for himself. He has variously been described as shy, unassuming, retiring and humble. Almost everybody who knew him made a point of how quiet he was in everything that he did. He was very modest and had no high opinion of his paintings. He just got on with things and left everybody else to get on with their lives. He could never have even contemplated trying to impose his will upon anybody else and was thus never angry. If he ever disapproved of something he never vocalised it, but instead a frown would appear across his brow.

An incident that took place at St Saviour's Episcopal Church, where Hugh worshipped, serves to illustrate his dislike of confrontation. It used to be the case that you could pay to reserve a seat in the church in order to help the church raise money. There were always more seats than there were people so seat rents were not in fact necessary. Eddie Orchard once sat on the pew reserved by a certain colonel. Hugh, going against his nature, but acting in accordance with duty, told Eddie that the seat was reserved and very politely asked him to move. Eddie wittily replied by saying that he had always thought the Lord's house was free to everybody. Hugh could not handle the situation, became very flustered and decided to let Eddie do as he pleased.

Hugh was very concerned with looking out for his friends and relatives. He was generous and always willing to help anybody who was in need. He was interested in everything and everybody. He always had a cheery word to say, had an 'absolutely lovely smile' and was never depressed. If he caught sight of you in the street he would tip his cap to acknowledge you. He was very charismatic and had an aura to him, but his charisma

5. *Fishing Boat, watercolour on paper, 375 x 500, collection of Molly Orchard.*

was entirely natural: it was completely unaffected and genuine. He was always very polite and courteous to everybody. Many of his friends have called him 'a right gentleman' or as one relative put it, he was 'old school'.

Hugh lived his life in a methodical manner. He appears to have liked routine. He lived in the same house, worshipped in the same church and had a single job for his entire life. He rarely did anything outgoing. The most outlandish events in his life were two trips he made abroad in the 1950s. In c.1956 he went on

holiday to Majorca with a couple, who lived in Bridge of Allan, and Norman and his wife Elizabeth. Roughly a year later he went on holiday to Ibiza with Mr and Mrs Flockhart, his friends from Bridge of Allan. He painted many pictures of the places he visited on these two trips (figs. 4 & 5). It is no wonder, given his character, that Hugh was well-respected by one and all. His relatives and friends all considered him to have been a 'very good man' and in Bridge of Allan he was thought of as a 'local worthy'.

HUGH GREEN AND ST SAVIOUR'S

Religion was extremely important to Hugh Green. He was a strong supporter of St Saviour's Church and everybody with a connection to the church knew him.

HUGH HAD A VERY DEEP FAITH and attended services at the church three times on Sundays. He went to prayers early in the morning, then worshipped at communion and later went to evensong. In the week he celebrated communion every morning.

He took on many responsibilities at the church. In 1915 he became the 'organ blower', whose job it was to work the organ's bellows. He was appointed to the vestry in 1918, a body of six people, who looked after the church's affairs. In Hugh's time it was the case that once someone attained a place on the vestry they stayed there for a long time. Other longstanding members, who knew Hugh, include Malcolm Allan, Ann McGregor and Eric Pullar. Hugh only left the vestry in 1953 after the church's constitution was changed. Members of the congregation decided that six new vestrymen should take over every three years, since it was felt that 'the management were becoming fossilized'. Hugh continued to welcome people into services after this and took the collection at evensong.

Hugh undertook all the exterior paint work for the church free of charge. He continued to carry out work for the church into his old age, even though by then he was quite frail. He was in the process of carrying out a job, the first stage of which involved stripping the old varnish off the pews, when he died. The congregation of St Saviour's honoured him for his work with an illuminated address, created by the artist Ailsa Craig (fig. 6).

The St Saviour's Annual Bazaar

Surprisingly, St Saviour's ended up being one of the many places Hugh Green exhibited his work. Sometime after John Shone became the rector in 1969 the church held annual sales of paintings to help raise funds. Some of the money raised from the sales went to St Saviour's and the rest was donated to the Stirling Children's Home. Apparently, Hugh Green had been so quiet about his artistic talents that many members of the congregation were unaware of them until he displayed his pictures at the first exhibition.

6. Illuminated Address by Ailsa Craig, 160 x 310, collection of Jean McLaren.

HUGH GREEN AS AN ARTIST

Hugh Green's Artistic Training

HUGH GREEN STUDIED at the Glasgow School of Art (GSA) in his early twenties.[6] He was not a full time student, but instead enrolled in evening classes in design, as many tradesmen of his generation did. It was a recognised route of developing skills and techniques in graining, marbling, wallpaper design, mixing of colours and sign-writing. Before attending the GSA he had in 1907 begun working with the Bridge of Allan painting and decorating partnership, P. & R. Rose.

The painter and stained glass designer, Robert Anning Bell (1863-1933), who was the Professor of Decorative Art at the GSA from 1911, probably oversaw the organisation of Hugh Green's classes. Bell was responsible for the Dorcas window in the west wall of St Saviour's. Dorcas was the woman in the Bible (Acts 9:36-41) who provided clothing for the poor and in whose name charitable organisations were founded. Hugh Green certainly would have known Bell through contemplating this window, if not through direct tuition. Bell also taught other Stirlingshire-resident artists Isobel Goudie, Ailsa Craig and Helen Lamb.

By the time Hugh Green began his studies at the GSA the School had acquired an international reputation for its excellence in the decorative arts. Francis Henry Newbery (1855-1946), appointed director of the School in 1885, vigorously promoted the applied arts over fine art. This fact must be considered in order to understand Hugh's artistic career. He studied in an environment in which interior decoration, which he ultimately pursued as a career, was considered on par with fine art. To see Hugh's work as a painter and decorator as entirely separate from his art would be to fall into the trap of a historical prejudice: the idea that craft is inferior to art.[7]

It was in Britain from the mid-nineteenth century that people involved in the arts sought to challenge this prejudice and raise the level of craft to that of art. The shift was referred to as the Arts and Crafts Movement. Its most influential pioneers were the designer, William Morris (1834-1896), and the theorist and critic, John Ruskin (1819-1900). Many of those, who promoted the movement, were responding to what they saw as the dehumanising effects of industrialisation and the beginnings of mass production with the division of labour. With specialisation, individuals were made to carry out repetitive tasks to create products. They were alienated from the objects they created, because they had no say over the aesthetic of the finished product. Ruskin claimed that people were effectively becoming soulless machines. He concluded: 'You must either make a tool of the creature, or a man of him. You cannot make both.'[8] Both Ruskin and Morris argued for a return to the Middle Ages, which they idealised as a period during which craftsmen were free agents and had control over the creative process. Morris claimed of the weavers and potters: '[t]here was little division of labour among them; …a man knew his work from end to end, and felt responsible for every stage of its progress.'[9]

Newbery, who was a great admirer of the work of Morris, helped to transform Glasgow into an international centre of the Arts and Crafts movement. He played a key role in bringing together a quartet of GSA students, who were to pioneer the so-called Glasgow Style. In c.1893 he introduced Charles

---

[6] The recent fire at the archives of the GSA has, for the moment, made it impossible to determine precisely when Hugh Green started his course. However, he was certainly a student from 1914-15, as he won a medal for textile design in this year.

[7] The origins of the prejudice can be traced to ancient Greek philosophical dualism: the idea that the mental sphere is superior to the material one. The dualism of the Greeks was revived in the Renaissance by Florentine humanists. Since then artists were promoted by the art establishment (namely the art academies) as people, who employed their intellects to endow their work with an underlying mental structure. Craftsmen, according to the establishment, merely employed their hands to manipulate material so their work was less worthy of consideration.

[8] John Ruskin. *The Stones of Venice: Volume II*. 2nd ed. (London: Smith, Elder and Co., 1867), 161.

[9] William Morris "Art, Wealth and Riches" *Manchester Quarterly* April, 1883. Quoted in Paul Thompson. *The Work of William Morris*. 3rd ed. (Oxford: Oxford University Press, 1991), 101.

Rennie Mackintosh (1868-1928) and Herbert McNair (1868-1955) to two sisters, Frances (1873-1921) and Margaret Macdonald (1864-1933), having noticed similarities in their styles. They became known as The Four and made it their mission to design everyday objects that combined utilitarianism with a concern for beauty. In 1902 Mackintosh (in a lecture entitled 'Seemliness') argued that 'the craftsman of the future must be an artist'.[10]

Mackintosh brought the Glasgow Style to Bridge of Allan at a time when Hugh Green was growing up. In 1895, whilst working for the Glasgow based partnership of Honeyman and Keppie, Mackintosh helped to design the no longer extant United Presbyterian Church, Bridge of Allan. At the time John Honeyman, one of the partners of the firm, was actually a resident of Bridge of Allan. The church was demolished in 1948 due to subsidence. Mackintosh undertook further work for the village in 1904, designing the pulpit, communion table, communion chairs, organ screen and choir stalls for Holy Trinity Church, located on the opposite side of Fountain Road to St Saviour's.

According to the testimony of Hugh Green's relatives he actually befriended Mackintosh whilst studying at the GSA.[11] In 1909 - probably not long before Hugh began

his studies - Mackintosh had overseen the completion of the construction of the GSA's iconic new building at 167 Renfrew Street. From 1910 until 1914 Mackintosh maintained a connection with the School as a member of its Board of Governors. Mackintosh must have thought highly of the young Hugh Green for he presented him with gifts, including a metal pig, which he had made out of strands of wire[12] as well as a number of sketches illustrating various techniques.[13] As well as Hugh Green, Mackintosh was in touch with other artists from Stirlingshire, including Henry (1870-1937) and Isobel Morley (1873-1948). He visited them at their home, The Gables, St Ninians. Crawford and Fraser of Stirling designed the house, which was completed in 1910, in an Arts and Crafts style.

Another Stirling Arts and Crafts development known to Hugh was that of Stirling Homesteads, a community of ten houses and cottages, built in 1910 on Crown land at the edge of Kings Park. Stirling Homesteads Ltd was set up by scientist Robert Maclaurin (1871 - 1948) who brought the Scottish Guild of Handicraft from Glasgow to Burghmuir, Stirling in 1909. The Guild was a co-operative partnership whose members produced art pottery, furniture, metalwork and stained glass. Their work was used in fitting out both the Homesteads and The Gables. The Stirling Smith has in its collection an oak cabinet featuring a floral gesso design, made by Henry T. Wyse for the Homesteads (fig. 7). Maclaurin was a member of the Stirling Circle of the Arts and Crafts, like the silversmith James A. Girvan (1895 – 1951), who (having spotted his talent in a GSA class) was persuaded to come and work in Stirling by gallery owner and GSA teacher John G. Mathieson.

7. Oak Cabinet designed by Henry T. Wyse, c.1910, collection of the Stirling Smith.

Another GSA teacher known to Hugh Green was Bridge of Allan born silversmith Peter Wylie Davidson (1870 – 1963) who for 38 years, until he retired in 1935, taught metalwork and wrote instruction books on metal and leatherworking. Davidson undertook commissions in the Stirling area, including the memorial plaque for the poet John Ferguson, made for the High School of Stirling, 1928, but now in the Smith's collections (fig. 8).

---

[10] C.R. Mackintosh, "Seemliness", 1902. Quoted in William Eadie. *Movements of Modernity: The Case of Glasgow and Art Nouveau.* (London: Routledge, 1990), 126.

[11] Hugh Green's nephew, Hugh, who was closest to him, recorded that he had actually been a student of Mackintosh. See Hugh Green, "Hugh Green" *St Saviour's Episcopal Church Newsletter* (1973). Whilst Mackintosh never held a formal teaching post at the GSA it is possible he may have given Hugh Green some tuition. Mackintosh certainly would not have known him in the capacity of a student, as he completed his studies in the year of Hugh Green's birth. Hugh Green's contact with Mackintosh must have been cut short by Mackintosh's move to England in July 1914.

[12] Hugh Green's niece, Norma Lunney, recalled admiring the wire model at Allanbank. Its current location is unknown.

[13] Hugh Green's nephew, Hugh, recorded that Hugh Green had showed him the sketches. Hugh Green, 1973, op. cit.

8. Commemorative Plaque for the poet John Ferguson, by Peter Wylie Davidson, 1928, collection of the Stirling Smith.

Hugh Green's Arts & Crafts Designs

Hugh Green created some beautiful designs for wallpaper and textiles whilst studying at the GSA. Interestingly his artwork does not share many similarities with the work of Mackintosh and that of other artists working in the Glasgow Style. None of his designs feature the flowing, complex, intertwined webs of lines found in Glasgow Style works. When Hugh Green was at the GSA the Glasgow Style was in fact just beginning to go out of fashion.

Some of Hugh Green's patterns are strikingly geometrical (fig. 9) and bear similarities with the work

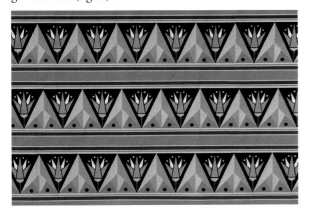

9. Geometric Pattern, body colour on paper, 560 x 2230, collection of Yvonne Syme.

of the Glasgow based designer Christopher Dresser (1834-1904). Dresser was a follower of the architect and designer Owen Jones (1809-1874). Green's sketchbooks evidence his familiarity with Jones' seminal reference book for designers, 'The Grammar of Ornament', published in 1856. Jones outlined what he thought to be the principles of the decorative arts in the book. It contains a great number of prints showing examples of ornament from different periods and cultures. Hugh Green copied many of the designs into a sketchbook, including several from the Egyptian section (fig. 10).

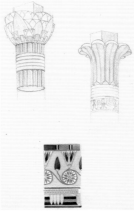

10. Studies copied from the Egyptian section of Jones' 'The Grammar of Ornament', graphite and watercolour on paper, 200 x 300, collection of Yvonne Syme.

11. Study of a Herald, graphite on paper, 155 x 250, collection of Yvonne Syme.

The sketchbook contains a number of stylised drawings of figures, including one of a herald bearing a trumpet and flag (fig. 11).

Green also carried out breath-taking floral designs at the GSA (figs. 12, 13, 14 & 15). They are similar in style to the less busy patterns created by Morris and his followers. His frieze depicting a hunting scene and

stylised oak leaves has echoes of the work of both John Moyr Smith and Walter Crane in the 1890s (fig. 16). As well as designs for wallpaper and textiles, Green made patterns for floor cloth or linoleum (fig. 17). Finally, he received traditional training in anatomy at the School.

12. Floral Pattern, body colour on paper, 780 x 780, collection of Yvonne Syme.

13. Floral Design for Print, body colour on paper, 270 x 390, collection of Yvonne Syme.

16. Hunting Scene, body colour on paper, 590 x 1940, collection of Yvonne Syme.

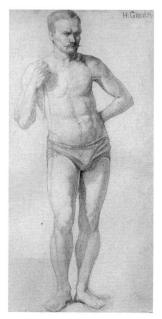

14. Floral Design for Print, body colour on paper, 270 x 360, collection of Yvonne Syme.

15. Floral Design for Print, body colour on paper, 310 x 410, collection of Yvonne Syme.

17. Floor Cloth Design, body colour on paper, 205 x 285, collection of Yvonne Syme.

18. Figure Study, graphite on paper, 380 x 560, collection of Yvonne Syme.

19. Medal: 'Evening School Award for Excellent Work' for textile design for the year 1914-15, collection of Yvonne Syme.

He executed detailed figure studies, which demonstrate a thorough understanding of the muscular structure of the human form (fig. 18).

The tutors at the GSA must have been highly impressed by Hugh Green's portfolio, for he was presented with an 'Evening School Award for Excellent Work' for textile design for the year 1914-15 (fig. 19). He also won a scholarship from the School to study in London, but never took up the offer.[14] His father died in 1913 and he had to give up his studies in order to support his mother and seven siblings.

The Stirling Circle of the Arts & Crafts

After his GSA training Hugh Green continued to develop his artistic talents by joining in with the activities of the Stirling Circle of the Arts and Crafts. Hugh was involved with the club from its earliest days. The first ever meeting of the club was held on 19 October 1928. His name first appears in the minutes of the club's first AGM, held on 5 April 1929, during which he was appointed to the committee. Herbert M. Nairn was the club's first president and Eric Sinclair Bell FRIBA, FRIAS (1884-1973), who was a practicing architect by profession, designed the club's logo (fig. 20). The first honorary president was the esteemed artist Sir D.Y. Cameron, whilst the honorary vice presidents were the well-known Stirlingshire artists William Walker ARE (1878-1961)[15] and John G. Mathieson (1880-1954).[16]

The club's original name indicates its commitment to promoting the Arts and Crafts ideal that objects used in everyday life should not only be functional, but also beautiful. The honorary vice president, William Walker, defended this view in several lectures he delivered to members of the club. For instance, on 6 October 1933 he gave a talk entitled 'The Arts and Crafts and

20. Logo of the Stirling Circle of the Arts and Crafts, Stirling Art Club Archives.

Everyday Life' at the Smith Institute (now the Stirling Smith). He had 'a few delightful and sound suggestions' to help the club to 'add to the joy of everyday life through artistic expression'.[17] Many of the talks focused on the applied arts as opposed to fine art. For instance, Thomas Callander Campbell Mackie (1886-1952), Head of the School of Design at the GSA, delivered a lecture on 18 March 1932 on 'Interior Decoration'. He discussed new ideas on functionalism, illustrating his talk with slides of New York skyscrapers and steel chairs.[18] Unfortunately by 1953 this initial enthusiasm for craft, which had captured the imaginations of artists throughout Scotland at the beginning of the century, had waned. In that year the club's name was changed to the Stirling Art Club and the logo was redesigned.

Events at the Stirling Circle

The general pattern of events at the club was established at the first committee meeting held on 2 November 1928 in the YMCA Rooms. It was agreed to meet on

---

[14] A niece of the artist, Jean McLaren, was told this by her uncle Robert Gordon (the second husband of Hugh Green's sister, Ella).

[15] The Stirling Smith has a significant collection of works by William Walker.

[16] The Stirling Smith has a collection of works by John Mathieson.

[17] "Artist's Helpful Address to Arts and Crafts Circle," *Stirling Sentinel*, October, 1933. Quoted in Stirling Art Club Minute Book 1928-1938, op. cit.

[18] "Stirling Circle of Arts and Crafts," *unknown paper*, March, 1932. Quoted in Stirling Art Club Minute Book 1928-1938, op. cit.

21. Hugh Green sketching, image provided by Ian Anderson.

alternate Fridays throughout the winter and spring. In the summer club members would meet every Saturday afternoon to attend outdoor sketching trips (figs. 21 & 22). The first sketching season ran from 4 May - 28 September 1929. The club also made visits to galleries to learn from other artists' work, including the National Gallery in Edinburgh, Kelvingrove Art Gallery and the Smith Institute.

22. Hugh Green sketching, image provided by The Dr Welsh Educational and Historical Trust.

The meetings in the winter included lectures, competitions, social gatherings and nights during which members' sketches were criticised by a practising artist. Life classes were introduced to the winter series at the end of the 1950s. The lecturers talked on a wide array of subjects including, to name a few, interior design, architecture, illumination, cinema, stained glass, etching, engraving, colour, draughtsmanship and modern art. The quality of the speakers at the club was extremely high. The club often recruited staff from the GSA to give talks, including the principal, Sir William Oliphant Hutchison RSA, ARSA, PSRA (1889-1970). Well-known practising artists such as James McIntosh Patrick RSA (1907-1998) and Thomas Symington Halliday MBE, FRSA (1902-1998) also delivered talks.

Competition nights were held regularly throughout the winter and appear to have been a popular feature of the winter syllabus. Hugh Green regularly won prizes at them. An example from 26 January 1934 will serve to illustrate the usual procedure. On that particular evening, J.C. Robson, acting as the 'master of ceremonies', challenged the members to sketch: 1) a street sloping down-hill; 2) a scene with a hill, loch and trees in the style of (a) 1834 and (b) 1934; 3) a Mickey

Mouse cartoon with four scenes; 4) Macbeth and the witches. Members voted for the best artworks and Hugh Green came second in the men's competition to J.C. Robson. Apparently some members had confused Macbeth with Tam o' Shanter.[19]

James Atterson (1898-1961), who for a long time was the art master at Stirling High School, regularly criticised members' sketches in the winter season. Atterson was an extremely talented graphic artist.

[19] Minute of January 26, 1934. Stirling Art Club Minute Book 1928-1938, op. cit.

23. Stirling Observer Christmas Number 1937, cover image designed by James Atterson, collection of the Stirling Smith.

24. James Atterson with the murals he painted for the Tourist Board Centre.

He designed bold images for a wide array of publications including brochures for the tourist industry, Sunday school handbooks and Stirling Observer annuals (fig. 23). He also painted striking murals promoting Stirling as 'the heart of Scotland', which were displayed in the temporary exhibition space at the Tourist Board Centre in Edinburgh in 1956 (fig. 24). He designed stained glass windows commemorating pupils of his school who had died in the two World Wars.

Exhibitions

Each year the club held an exhibition and a dinner. The club's first exhibition was held from 12-14 December 1929 at the Windsor Hall, 12 Port Street (fig. 25). Hugh Green was appointed to the hanging committee before the club's first exhibition in 1929 and served on it with dedication for many subsequent years. He exhibited seven works at the first exhibition, but did not put any of them up for sale. His work received praise from two journalists who reviewed the exhibition. One wrote: 'His works are quite outstanding having a peculiar style all his own.'[20] Another reported: 'The exhibits of Mr Hugh Green revealed merit, his 'Street Corner' being a thing of delight.'[21] In subsequent exhibitions Hugh Green put his works up for sale. They proved extremely popular and sold in large numbers.

Another exhibitor at the first Stirling Circle exhibition was David McKee. Hugh Green and David were good friends and used to attend the club's sketching trips together. Hugh used to visit David at the family home at Lecropt Cottage, Bridge of Allan. David's son got to know Hugh as a boy. He lived and worked abroad, but returned to Bridge of Allan sometime after Hugh had died. Upon his return to Bridge of Allan, one of Hugh's relatives gave him a sketchbook as a memento, which contained beautiful pictures of Stirlingshire (fig. 26).

The objects displayed at the club's exhibitions demonstrate the club's commitment to the Arts and Crafts movement. Hand crafted everyday objects of all sorts, such as chess sets, model ships, kitchen utensils,

[20] "Arts and Crafts Exhibition," *unknown paper,* December, 1929. Quoted in Stirling Art Club Minute Book 1928-1938, op. cit.

[21] "Stirling Circle of Arts and Crafts," *unknown paper,* December, 1929. Quoted in Stirling Art Club Minute Book 1928-1938, op. cit.

tools, clothes accessories, pottery and silverware, were regularly displayed (figs. 27 & 28). Sir D.Y. Cameron sent some beautifully crafted objects from his own personal collection to the second exhibition in November 1930. He supplied a claret jug made by Edward Spencer, a glazed pot created by the Martin Brothers and some

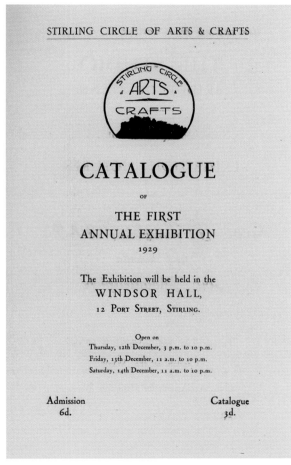

25. The catalogue of the first exhibition of the Stirling Circle of the Arts and Crafts, Stirling Art Club Archives.

26. *Cottage, watercolour on paper, 120 x 175, collection of Carole McKee.*

27. *Members of the Stirling Circle at the sixth annual exhibition, Hugh Green, second from the right, Stirling Art Club Archives.*

at three-year intervals. In the 1940s Hugh Green also exhibited at the annual exhibitions of the Royal Glasgow Institute of the Fine Arts. In 1944 his painting 'In Harbour' was on show and in 1946 his picture of 'Craigforth Mill' was on display.

The Stirling Circle during World War II
The activities of the Stirling Circle were postponed during the Second World War. When the war broke out in September 1939 a circular was issued to club members informing them of the temporary closure of the club (fig. 29). The summer sketching trips were cancelled owing to government restrictions on sketching aimed at stopping spies from gathering visual data. The committee were informed by the police that if members of the club wished to sketch they would have to apply for permits. Members' work would have to be submitted for inspection. If they chose to sketch they would be doing so 'at their own risk'. The club's honorary president, Sir D.Y. Cameron died during the war. It was only in March 1946 that the committee met and agreed to renew the club's activities. It was shortly after the war that Hugh Green would be appointed to the important post of treasurer of the club.

wrought iron candlesticks and fire irons. Reviewing the 1936 exhibition one reporter wrote that the idea that art was not utilitarian was 'disproved in Stirling by the variety of articles of a useful and ornamental character on view.'[22]

[22] "Arts and Crafts," *Stirling Journal*, November, 1936. Quoted in Stirling Art Club Minute Book 1928-1938, op. cit.

As a member of the Stirling Circle, Hugh Green also sent his work to other local and national exhibitions. In 1938 he displayed two paintings, 'Winter' and 'Evening', at the final exhibition of the Stirling Fine Art Association. Alexander Croall (1804-1885), the Stirling Smith's first curator, and Leonard Baker, the art master of Stirling High School organised the first exhibition of the association in 1878 as a means of displaying work by contemporary practising artists. From then on, eighteen exhibitions were held at the Smith Institute, usually

28. *Members of the Stirling Circle at an exhibition, Hugh Green in the centre, Stirling Art Club Archives.*

From Committee Member to Honorary President

Hugh Green was thoroughly committed to the Stirling Circle and was involved with its activities right up until the time of his death. It would have been quite out of character for him to have sought out positions of authority for himself. However, his dedicated service was awarded with many offices. During a general meeting held on 30 April 1948 he was appointed treasurer. As he rose through the ranks of the club he became more vocal. The number of notes in the minute book that mention how he expressed thanks to various members of the club for the work they had done in a way that went beyond mere formalities, testify to his kindly character. He was later appointed vice president on 1 April 1955 at the AGM.

Hugh Green was eventually 'unanimously elected as president' at the AGM of 1956, held on 6 April. He took over as president at a time when the club had had a number of unsuccessful years. The exhibitions of the past two years had both made losses. In the minutes of the AGM of 1956 the minute secretary noted: 'About finance the president reported that the position was serious and required careful consideration.' The sketching trips had been poorly attended and the winter meetings of 1955 had had to be curtailed since the club had been unable to find a venue for them. Thankfully the club secured the Unionist Rooms for the 1956 winter lecture series. Hugh Green's presidency appeared to go well. Money was raised for the club through raffles and an increase in sales of pictures at the annual exhibition, making the treasurer's report at the AGM of 1957 a 'cheerful one' and solving the club's financial worries.

Hugh Green demitted office at the AGM of 1960 and returned to the committee. He was later honoured for his service to the club by being elected honorary vice-president at the AGM of 1962, held on 6 April. Despite no longer being under obligation to pay the club a membership fee, Hugh Green, in keeping with his generous character, continued to donate to the club

on a yearly basis. At the AGM of 1963 Hugh Green thanked the club for the appointment and expressed his wish to be with them more often. Throughout the sixties he acted as chairman at various meetings and was described in the minute book in glowing terms as 'a very highly esteemed member of the club'. Hugh Green was awarded the highest honour of the club on 5 April 1968, when he was elected honorary president at the AGM.

Dear Sir or Madam,

I have to advise you that owing to the outbreak of war, the committee has decided to suspend all activities of the club until further notice.

Yours faithfully,

Daisy Watt,
Secretary.

29. *Circular sent to Stirling Circle members, 1939, Stirling Art Club Archives.*

HUGH GREEN'S PAINTINGS

Despite having studied design at the GSA and joined the Stirling Circle, a club committed to the Arts and Crafts movement, Green devoted much of his time to painting relatively traditional landscapes.

HE NEVER EXHIBITED ANY DESIGN WORK with the Stirling Circle, but instead showed numerous paintings at almost every annual exhibition. He used his painting and decorating business as an outlet for his creative design talents and chose to pursue fine art in his free time. Green clearly did not see much of a division between the two. Whereas some artists upheld oils and canvas as the noblest materials, Green was never so snobbish. He only rarely painted in oil on canvas (fig. 30). He often used house paints and was happy to use any material as a surface, including discarded pieces of wallpaper (fig. 31). An exposition of some of the most characteristic features of his paintings follows.

Clarity & Precision

The way in which as an artist he managed to give even the most complicated composition an air of calmness and clarity is one of the most remarkable aspects of his style. Journalists reporting on the Stirling Circle's annual exhibitions often commented on this aspect of his work. Over the years journalists marvelled at the 'very thoughtful and precise' quality of his paintings, the 'Breton-like calm' of his work, the 'serene quality' of his watercolours and his ability to produce 'clear, clean pictures'.

30. The Old Airthrey Paper Mill, oil on canvas, 1912, 280 x 415, collection of Yvonne Syme.

31. Sunset over Stirling, watercolour on card, 1930, collection of Yvonne Syme.

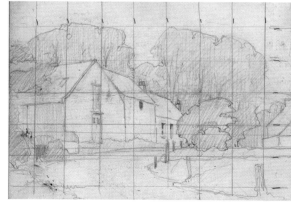

32. Sunset over Stirling, watercolour on card, 1930, collection of Yvonne Syme.

33. Lecropt Kirk, watercolour on paper, 1969, 245 x 345, collection of Molly Orchard.

34. Airthrey Paper Mill, body colour on paper, 320 x 485, collection of The Stirling Smith

One journalist was even mildly critical of this aspect of his work:

'Hugh Green in his works, strives to get a clear, clean effect … However, in trying to maintain the clear, transparent effect, one felt he had detracted from the appeal of 'Old Brig, Stirling,' in painting it in light colours, fawns and browns, which made it look more like a new construction than a landmark which has weathered many hundreds of historic years.'[23]

Green lived a thoughtful life and was methodical in everything he did: from the way he dressed to the way he organised his life around fixed routines. His working methods in painting are no exception. He used to sketch outdoors and then take his sketches home with him. He created paintings based on these sketches in his flat, sometimes meticulously superimposing grids on them to transfer the images precisely (fig. 32). He seems to have been of the opinion that there was a clear difference between a sketch and a finished painting. He often painted the same scenes over and over again. According to many relatives he was rarely satisfied with his paintings as they never met his exacting standards. The result of this approach is that many of his compositions are extremely similar, though they are never identical. His precision favoured certain subjects: his landscapes usually feature highly accomplished renderings of buildings (figs. 33 & 34). A journalist reporting on the 1954 Stirling Circle exhibition commended his 'mastery of architectural drawing'.[24]

Colour & Texture

In general, Green favoured using lighter, less saturated, pastel colours, resulting in pictures imbued with a feeling of calm and restfulness (fig. 35). Journalists often commented on the 'subtlety of colour and effect' in Hugh Green's paintings.[25]

[23] "Stirling Art Club Stages 23rd Annual Exhibition," *Stirling Observer*, October 25, 1960. Quoted in Stirling Art Club Minute Book 1938-1987. Stirling Art Club Archives. Victoria Place, Stirling.

[24] "Art Exhibition," *Stirling Observer*, November 16, 1954. Quoted in Stirling Art Club Minute Book 1938-1987, op. cit.

[25] "Arts and Crafts," *Stirling Observer*, November, 1937. Quoted in Stirling Art Club Minute Book 1928-1938, op. cit.

35. Ella and Norman Green in the Highlands, watercolour on paper, 1947, 480 x 325, collection of Jean McLaren.

36. Clydesdales, watercolour on paper, 345 x 470, collection of Jean McLaren.

One reporter praised his 'rare skill at rendering the faded colours and shadings of weather-beaten buildings' in his 'exquisite watercolours of Pittenween harbour'.[26] Another claimed that his painting of Stirling Castle, as viewed from Raploch farm, had 'an individual quality and a technique of subdued colouring which should attract'.[27]

Green's colouring is always distinguished by its cheerfulness and delicacy. His pictures are light, not only in the technical sense that his colours have a high value, but also in the sense that his colouring instils in viewers a feeling of lightness of heart. One journalist claimed that Green's painting of the lily pond at Polmaise exhibited a 'delicacy of colour and gaiety of feeling'. The reporter contrasted this feature of his work to the 'sense of weight that is like Cézanne' found in a painting of the same subject by Miss M. Mackintosh.[28]

A number of Green's paintings do feature slightly darker, over-saturated colours, so that (as one of his friends remarked) they bear a resemblance to 1930s railway station posters (fig. 36). Hugh Green's painting and decorating workshop walls were pasted with old posters, having been put there by a former employee. Perhaps Hugh Green was influenced by them. He

[26] "Art Exhibition," *Stirling Observer*, November 16, 1954. Quoted in Stirling Art Club Minute Book 1938-1987, op. cit.

[27] "Stirling Exhibition," *Stirling Journal*, November, 1933. Quoted in Stirling Art Club Minute Book 1928-1938, op. cit.

[28] "Arts and Crafts," *Stirling Observer*, November 13, 1951. Quoted in Stirling Art Club Minute Book 1938-1987, op. cit.

37. Jack Merriott tutoring at one of the Stirling Circle's sketching trips on the banks of the Teith, Stirling Art Club Archives.

may have also been inspired by the work of the artist Jack Merriott (1904-1968), who designed many iconic British Railways posters. Merriott gave instruction at the Stirling Circle's summer sketching outings in both 1952 and 1953. In May 1953 club members met in the grounds of Doune Castle, where Merriott gave them tuition (fig. 37). Hugh Green painted several pictures of the castle, which he may have carried out during this visit (fig. 38). Merriott showed two paintings in the Stirling Circle's 1952 exhibition, one of which may have been the view of Stirling Bridge, recently acquired by the Stirling Smith (fig. 39). Merriott was offered the position of honorary president of the club in 1956. When he accepted the offer, Green, as president of the club, called him to personally thank him and express the club's 'pride and pleasure'.

The texture of the paint in Green's artworks differs from one picture to another. In some paintings he made very little use of opaque paint (fig. 40). He layered transparent paint on light surfaces in a traditional manner to create the darks. He left the light colour of the paper or card showing in the places he wanted highlights. In such paintings he occasionally placed opaque highlights on top of darks where necessary (fig. 41). In other paintings he used opaque paint almost entirely. In such pictures

39. The Bridge, Stirling, watercolour on paper, 380 x 480, collection of the Stirling Smith.

there is little contrast between transparent and opaque paint so that the surface of the picture plane is emphasised (fig. 42). Such paintings appear flat, which brings out the decorative qualities of the shapes of the objects depicted in them.

Water & Reflections

An assessment of Green's artistic output would not be complete without mention of his aptitude for representing water and reflections. His treatment of water regularly received praise from journalists visiting the Stirling Circle's annual exhibitions. One reporter noted that '…the gently swelling, reflection-filled river is vividly portrayed' in his picture of Allanbank (fig. 43).[29] Another journalist commented on the 'beauty and

38. Doune Castle, watercolour on paper, 275 x 365, collection of Yvonne Syme.

[29] "Local Art Makes a Show," *Stirling Observer*, November 22, 1934. Quoted in Stirling Art Club Minute Book 1938-1987, op. cit. The picture was printed in the catalogue of the 1934 exhibition. It closely resembles other compositions created by Hugh Green of the same scene.

40. Study of a Tree, watercolour on paper, 1959, 370 x 505, collection of Yvonne Syme.

41. Stirling Castle, watercolour on paper, 1962, 255 x 350, collection of The Stirling Smith

quiet tone' of a 'dream-view' of Stirling reflected in the Forth.[30] One article contained the conclusive paragraph:

> **'No artist in the exhibition excels Mr Hugh Green, Bridge of Allan, in his treatment of water studies. 'Fishing Boats, Dunmore' is one of the best of these. Shadow and surface ripple are splendidly depicted, and the artist has been successful in infusing an atmosphere of Breton-like calm into the picture. 'Old Bridge, Stirling' is a true-to-life study and here again the water's treatment is arresting.'[31]**

The Allan Water is the defining feature of Bridge of Allan and was for many years the life blood of the village, powering its numerous mills. Green's home overlooked the river and he must have spent much time watching it flow past his window.

Hugh Green as a Copyist

Hugh Green was very interested in history. He recorded facts about various old local shops and industries in his sketchbooks. On a page of one sketchbook he drew a detailed, annotated map, which indicated the locations of remnants of the Airthrey Copper Mine. He also made several paintings showing what Bridge of Allan might have looked like in the past. At some point he had been given the job of repainting the interior of the burgh chambers. Whilst undertaking the job he discovered a painting in a naïve style showing a shop owned by John Campbell on the left, a butcher's known as 'Josephine Cottage' in the centre and the Toll Bar on the right (fig. 44). The painting was in very bad condition so Green decided to make a copy of it (fig. 45). He made several smaller copies of the painting, though none of them have come to light.

---

[30] "Arts Exhibition," *Stirling Journal*, November 20, 1930. Quoted in Stirling Art Club Minute Book 1928-1938, op. cit.

[31] "Stirling Exhibition," *unknown paper*, November, 1932. Quoted in Stirling Art Club Minute Book 1928-1938, op. cit.

42. Hillfoots Village, body colour on paper, 370 x 480, collection of The Stirling Smith

44. The Old Toll House, oil on canvas, mid-nineteenth century, collection of the Dr Welsh Trust.

43. Allanbank by Hugh Green from the 1934 Stirling Circle exhibition catalogue, Stirling Art Club Archives.

45. (right) The Old Toll House, watercolour on watercolour board, collection of the Dr Welsh Trust.

AT BRIDGE OF ALLAN   *Hugh Green*

The painting depicts an important aspect of Bridge of Allan's history. The toll house was constructed at the end of the eighteenth century. Money was collected from those crossing the bridge to pay for its maintenance and that of the surrounding roads. Some drovers crossed the river further down at the ford to avoid paying the tolls. The toll house used to be situated at the east end of the old bridge (constructed in 1520) on the south side of the original road that ran through the village. The old bridge crossed the Allan Water in a north-easterly direction and the road carried on in that direction. Henderson Street was only constructed in 1809 when the marshy ground was drained. The toll house was demolished at the end of the nineteenth century, when tolls were phased out. The stone gate post, which supported the toll gate on the north side of the road, still survives. It is known as the Toll Bar stone and can be visited by following a footpath on the north side of the road to the east of the bridge.

The bridge is at the heart of the village's story. Locals, including Green himself, sometimes referred to the village as 'The Brig'. It is not surprising that Hugh Green made several copies of a picture depicting the bridge in times gone by (fig. 46). He based his paintings on a print, contained in the book 'By Allan Water' by Katherine Steuart (fig. 47). The image is a picturesque rendering of the old bridge, constructed in 1520. The book tells the story of the house (constructed in 1600) at the east end of the bridge. James Steuart, an ancestor of the author, bought the house and turned it into an inn. He was known as 'The Paip'. The farm he came from on the edge of the River Tay was called 'Rome', since Roman artefacts had been discovered near to it. He claimed to be a descendant of King James II of Scotland. Unsurprisingly he was a supporter of the Jacobites and the local lairds often met in the inn to devise plots to put the House of Stewart back on the throne.

46. *The Old Bridge, watercolour on paper, 370 x 480, collection of The Stirling Smith.*

Painting & Photography

Green's self-effacing character has already been noted. He does not seem to have been interested in imposing his will upon others or the world around him. Similarly, he was unconcerned with projecting his personal emotions onto his pictures, but was instead preoccupied with recording visual facts. This aspect of his work prevents him from being labelled a Romantic, even if he shared the Romantics' love of nature. Perhaps it also explains his keen interest in photography, a medium often considered to be capable of capturing objective facts.

Green was a member of a photography group based in Bridge of Allan. He constructed a pinhole camera at a time when cheap mass-produced cameras were unavailable. He took photographs with it, including one of his mother standing in the kitchen of Allanbank (fig. 48). The Stirling Circle also held events promoting the medium of photography. Hugh Green was on the committee which agreed to buy a projector for the club in September 1931. In March 1939 a demonstration of Agfacolour and Dufacolour photographic transparencies was put on by club members. The club also held events on moving pictures. For instance, in November

47. Print of the old bridge from 'By Allan Water' by Katherine Steuart.

48. Photograph taken by Hugh Green of his mother in the kitchen in Allanbank.

49. Portrait of Hugh Green by George Hughes.

1938 James S. Nairn, manager of the Regal Cinema, along with James Atterson showed some five films, four of which they had made themselves, to members of the club.

Green took a great number of photographs using 35mm colour film of the local area and of the scenery he encountered on his holidays to Majorca and Ibiza. He showed some slides of holiday scenes he had taken in Majorca at one of the Stirling Circle's 'film nights' in January 1957. Colour film must have been something of a novelty then. A reporter joked that club members would be replacing 'brush and palette with camera and Kodachrome'.[32] Green often used photography in the process of creating paintings. He would usually sketch from life then take a photograph of the scene in front of him. His nephew, Norman Graham, projected slides of the photographs he had taken onto the wall for him. Green then used to look at the projected images for colour reference.

[32] "Stirling Observer Art Club Hold Annual Social Evening", *unknown paper,* April 4, 1957. Quoted in Stirling Art Club Minute Book 1938-1987, op. cit.

Green was friends with the accomplished photographer, George J. Hughes FRPS, who was a fellow member of the Stirling Circle. In an advertisement for one of Hughes' exhibitions, placed in the catalogue of the Stirling Circle's first exhibition, it was claimed that

50. Field of Flowers, watercolour on paper, 370 x 495, collection of Yvonne Syme.

Hugh Green's Paintings & Modernism

During Hugh Green's lifetime some of the most dramatic changes ever occurred in the visual arts. The art promoted by major galleries in 1973 would not have been recognised as art in 1892. Amidst such change, Hugh Green remained conservative. A journalist reporting on the 1934 exhibition referred to him as an 'orthodox' artist.[33] Whilst some members of the Stirling Circle exhibited progressive, abstract works at the annual exhibitions, the majority of the members of the club displayed traditional work. Generally journalists reporting on the Stirling Circle's exhibitions were relieved to see this trend. They denigrated modern art labelling it with derogatory terms including 'puzzling', 'utterly incomprehensible' and 'freakish'.[34]

However, the club members certainly had a good awareness of trends in modern art and various talks were devoted to the issue. For instance, in March 1931 T.S. Campbell Mackie gave a talk on modern art. He spoke of how science, rapid transport and the power of the press had all influenced the course of art. Other lectures were less objective and more partisan. Mr P. Smyth of the Alloa Academy argued that the public were too often tricked into thinking that 'some hideous blobs of colour or distorted figures are the works of genius...'[35]

[33] "Arts and Crafts", *Stirling Journal,* November 22, 1934. Quoted in Stirling Art Club Minute Book 1928-1938, op. cit.

[34] Terms such as 'freakish' were often used to describe modern art. Their origins can be traced to the end of the 19th century, when writers such as Max Nordau claimed that modern art was a symptom of degeneration. The idea that mankind was undergoing a process of degeneration - the reverse of Darwinian evolution – was widespread and was supported by well-known figures including H.G. Wells.

[35] "Stirling Circle of Arts and Crafts," *unknown paper,* February, 1932. Quoted in Stirling Art Club Minute Book 1928-1938, op. cit.

Hughes had won over 150 awards for high class work and that his photographs had been shown in 'all the capitals of the world'. From 1921 Hughes owned a shop on Union Street called 'The Studio', located just behind Hugh Green's workshop. The building it was based in survives today. Green used to visit Hughes regularly and pose as a subject for his photographs. He took a photo of Hugh in a smock, with a painting in the background depicting his sisters Ella and May as young children (fig. 49). Hughes was awarded a prize for the photograph, having entered it into a competition. Green attached prints of the photograph to the reverse of many of his paintings.

Arguably, however, there is a modern note in Green's work, even if they are by and large conservative. The well-known art critic, Clement Greenberg (1909-1994), claimed that two-dimensionality was the essential quality of painting. He argued that the flatness of the picture plane was especially evident in work created by modern artists. For him modern paintings were superior to compositions, which created the illusion of space.

Until the 19th century artists sought to make a flat surface appear like an 'open window'.[36] They either employed line, known as 'disegno', or tonal modelling, known as 'colore' to achieve this end. Lines help viewers by providing them with information not usually available through the sense of sight, namely that certain objects are separate from each other. Tonal modelling makes objects appear three-dimensional.

Hugh Green made limited use of line and tonal modelling. The flatness of the picture surface is evident as a result. Shapes and colours can be appreciated for their aesthetic value, rather than just being seen as representative of objects, making his pictures 'finely decorative' as one journalist put it (figs. 50 & 51).[37] Perhaps Green's training as a designer influenced him to paint in this way.

---

[36] The Western idea of a painting as an 'open window' was famously pronounced by the Florentine humanist, Leon Battista Alberti (1404-1472), in his 'On Painting' of 1435.

[37] "Arts and Crafts Exhibition," *unknown paper,* November, 1930. Quoted in Stirling Art Club Minute Book 1928-1938, op. cit.

51. Lesley Pullar, Elizabeth Graham and Yvonne Graham, watercolour on paper, 1960, 360 x 510, collection of Yvonne Syme.

ART, GOD AND NATURE

Hugh Green's nephew, Hugh, who was closest to him and knew him best, wrote that he lived for two things: 'art and the joys of nature' and 'God and his fellow man'.

HE REPUTEDLY HAD AN 'AMAZING KNOWLEDGE' of nature.[38] To suggest that Hugh Green, as a disciple of God and lover of nature, was celebrating human joy in God's creation through his work, is an idea that logically coheres with the available facts. Christian thinkers have for centuries conceptualised God as an artist and nature as his artwork.[39] Renaissance Neo-Platonists considered the cosmos to be ordered according to the ideas of God. They merged the Platonic notion that the universe is divided into an ideal, perfect 'mental' sphere and an imperfect, changeable, material realm with the Christian divisions between Heaven and Earth, Faith and Sin. The material world was seen to have an underlying mental order.

Green's artworks appear to capture the spirit of this Christian notion of the universe as a structured artwork. The design work he executed at the GSA orders colours and shapes - the raw material - according to the mental principles of harmony, symmetry and balance. Meanwhile his landscapes and townscapes are light, clear, structured, ordered and beautiful. Resting

one's eyes upon an artwork by Green is a calming and sobering experience. One journalist reporting on the Stirling Circle's 1937 exhibition used the phrase 'mystical atmosphere' to describe a painting of Stirling Castle.[40] For the journalist the painting was imbued with spirituality and this is no surprise given Green's commitment to the Christian faith.

As a painter and decorator Green certainly would not have agreed with the belief of artists of the Aesthetic movement that 'all art is useless', as Oscar Wilde put it. However, he may have agreed with their idea that beauty can be found in the form - the arrangement of shapes and colours - not just the content of an artwork. When Green was growing up the so-called Glasgow Boys were working in and around Bridge of Allan. The Boys were inspired by figures in the Aesthetic movement such as James Abbott McNeill Whistler (1834-1903) and took on the idea that paintings could have underlying harmonic structures like musical compositions.

William Kennedy (1859-1918), lived in Cambuskenneth, just south-east of Bridge of Allan, from 1885 until 1898. Various other Boys, including E.A. Walton and George Henry used to visit him there. Green would not have reached the age of ten when Kennedy moved away. However, he may have crossed paths with William York MacGregor (1855-1923), the so-called 'father' of the group, who retired to Bridge of Allan on his return from South Africa at the beginning of the 1890s. He was buried at Old Logie Kirkyard, just along the road from where Green himself would be laid to rest years later.

Finally, Green avoids darkness and obscurity in his work at all costs. Such qualities have been cited by Christian philosophers as ones, which instil in people a sense of 'the sublime', namely a sense of awe in God's terrible power as expressed in nature. Hugh Green's personal religiosity was not centred on an Old Testament 'fire and brimstone' conception of God as a powerful, aloof higher being. He must have thought of God in terms of his New Testament manifestation as Christ. In any case, he certainly devoted his life to following Christ's example of loving God and humanity.

---

[38] Hugh Green, 1973, op. cit.

[39] Dante Alighieri (c.1265-1321) in Canto XI of his Inferno wrote: 'Philosophy points out to who will learn,/How Nature takes her course from the Sublime/Intellect and Its Art;'

[40] "Stirling Circle's Success," *Stirling Observer*, November, 1937. Quoted in Stirling Art Club Minute Book 1928-1938, op. cit.

HUGH GREEN'S PAINTING AND DECORATING BUSINESS

Hugh Green was able to express his own individual creativity not only by painting pictures in his spare time, but also through his work as an interior decorator.

HE BEGAN WORKING as a painter and decorator in 1907, having joined the partnership of the brothers, Peter and Robert Rose. He enjoyed his work and remained a painter and decorator for his entire life.

During his career Green undertook many civic painting commissions including the Fountain of Nineveh, the interior of the Burgh Chambers on Henderson Street and the Paterson Clock. The clock was named after Alexander Paterson, a well-known and well-respected botanist. He also repainted the provost's lamp several times. In Green's day the lamp used to be relocated every time there was a new provost to a spot in front of the provost's house. It is now permanently located in a park at the junction between Henderson Street, Alexander Drive and Union Street.

Green also painted many of the interiors and exteriors of houses in Bridge of Allan. He was usually happy to carry out special commissions to decorate interiors on request. He once decorated the interior of the surgery in Fountain Road, the work place of Dr Walker, a fellow member of the congregation of St Saviour's. Green considered the results of the paint job a little bland, so he gave the doctor two paintings to enliven the walls.

Green was a skilled sign writer. Amongst the many jobs he carried out was a sign for the Lady of the Lake Hotel, which he had to paint in reverse on a sheet of glass. He created many house name signs, including that of 'Tanglin', 3 Well Road, Bridge of Allan (the home of Provost William Steel) in the 1950s. He executed the design in gold lettering on the black lintel of the main entrance.

Green also supplied and put up wallpaper. He sometimes designed it and had it printed. His niece, Joan (the daughter of Green's brother James), recalled being given wallpaper to cover their school jotters. At Christmas she and her siblings used to visit Green's workshop. He gave them old wallpaper sample books to make paper chains out of to decorate their house.

The History of P. & R. Rose

Green recounted the history of P. & R. Rose in a document he left in the Dr Welsh Trust. The company were first based in Finsbury Cottage, which was situated next to the Royal Hotel on Henderson Street. James Gray owned the cottage at the time. The partnership later moved to 28 Henderson Street.[41] In the late nineteenth century the workshop was relocated to Queen's Lane

and the premises on Henderson Street were retained as an office and showroom until 1935.

When Green joined the firm one of the partners, Peter, had already died in 1904. His brother, Robert, subsequently died in 1919. Robert's son, William P. Rose, took over the business, but he died only a year later. From then on Green formed a partnership with William's daughters, Margaret, Alice and Helen Rose. The Roses attended to the business side, whilst Green carried out the actual painting and decorating work. In 1943, when Margaret, Alice and Helen retired, Hugh Green took over the business in his own name as 'Hugh Green House Painter and Decorator'. His sister, May, carried out all the paperwork for him. He retired not long after he returned from a holiday in Ibiza in c.1958. After that he would oblige people, but he no longer undertook any major jobs.

Hugh Green's Workshop

Hugh Green's workshop was situated in a building on Queen's Lane (fig. 52). Robertson and Ramsay, Joiners owned the building and used part of it as a workshop. A friend of Green's, Ian Anderson, used to work for them. He grew up in the house next to Allanbank, which burnt down. He served his apprenticeship with Robertson and

---

[41] In 1970 the premises was occupied by a shop with the name 'Kays Ladies & Baby Ware'.

52. Hugh Green's workshop, image provided by Ian Anderson.

Ian recalled that the workshop on Queen's Lane had three floors. Robertson and Ramsay were an undertaker's as well as a joiner's and Ian used to make coffins for them, which were stored on the top floor of the building. In fact, the firm actually carried out the undertaking of many members of Green's family, including that of Green himself. There were two entrances to the building. It could be accessed from Union Street or from the bottom of Queen's Lane. The houses on Union Street used to back onto the workshop's yard. Robertson and Ramsay were based in rooms on the Union Street side of the building and Hugh Green's workshop was on the ground floor on the Queen's Lane side. Ian recalled playing on a penny farthing bicycle in Queen's Lane as a boy.

The walls of Green's workshop were covered with old posters advertising the railways, Great War recruitment posters and prints, which John McLaren had put up. John had grown up in Bridge of Allan and began an apprenticeship with P. & R. Rose in 1877. He worked for them for forty years, married and raised a son and daughter in the village. One wall of Green's workshop was covered in layers of dried paint that looked like molten lava. Over the years, painters had cleaned their brushes on the wall to stop them from hardening.

The old fire station was next to the workshop in Queen's Lane. Hugh Green stored some of his equipment there. He used a barrow to transport his equipment to the place he was undertaking a job. The barrow was beautifully decorated, as it functioned as a means of advertising Hugh Green's signwriting skills. He had painted it in 'mushroom', a favourite colour of the time. The details were painted in a lighter shade of mushroom and the lettering was painted in black. He could be seen walking around the village in a pair of overalls wheeling the barrow along. It took two men to wheel the barrow up the hill. Hugh Green sometimes went to Leith Walk in Edinburgh to buy the paint he used. He carried the pots of paint he had bought home with him on the bus.

Before Robertson and Ramsay bought the workshop it had been owned by J. McKay McGregor. According to Green himself, he had been the postmaster at Bridge of Allan until his retirement and was secretary to The Strathallan Meeting (now The Bridge of Allan Highland Games) for over fifty years. J. McKay had inherited the workshop from his father, William McGregor. William had been a partner in the firm of McGregor & Eadie, Joiners, who helped to build some of what Green referred to as the 'fine Victorian houses' in Bridge of Allan.

After Hugh Green left the workshop William Miller took it over and continued to use it for his painting and decorating business, William Miller & Sons. Until then William Miller & Sons were based on Henderson Street. Both the workshop and the fire station were later torn down in order to build new blocks of flats, which have since been demolished to make way for even newer flats. Ian Anderson mentioned that the village used to be a third of the size it is now when he was a boy.

Ramsay before joining the army aged twenty-one. He then worked for the RAF in air traffic control in Malta and Libya before returning to Bridge of Allan. Robertson and Ramsay took him on again upon his return and he worked with them for ten to twelve years.

Ian later took a job as a joiner with Kork-n-Seal and worked with them until he was sixty-one. The company manufactured closures for bottles and caps for jars. The factory was established in Bridge of Allan in 1938 on the site of the Pullar's Kierfield works, which by then had been shut down. United Closures and Plastics (UCP), part of Global Closure Systems, now own the factory. They used to employ around 1200 people and provided accommodation for all the workers. One of Ian's main jobs was sorting out the problem of dry rot in the workers' houses. Now the company have far fewer employees, or as Ian put it, computers do not need a tea break, they do not smoke and they do not need to use the toilet! Ian was also a member of the Bridge of Allan fire brigade.

HUGH GREEN'S LOVE OF MUSIC

Hugh Green loved music as well as art.
He owned a wind-up gramophone, which was equipped with a 'monster horn'.

APPARENTLY HE PLAYED 78s on it so loudly that it used to sound as if you were standing in the orchestra pits when you listened to it. Green collected thorns from bushes and shaped them so that he could use them as needles. He preferred them to the metal needles supplied with the gramophone as they wore down the shellac from which the records were made. He also owned a radio, which was powered with an old lead-acid battery. He had to refill the glass jars of the battery with acid from time to time. Only using the radio a little would take a lot of battery power.

Green was also an accomplished violinist, a skill which he had learnt entirely on his own without tuition (fig. 53). Willie also used to play the violin, but he called it the fiddle. Hugh Green played classical music, but Willie used to play popular folk songs. Hugh and Willie used to practise in their flat in Allanbank. Eddie Orchard often heard them playing from his flat. On hearing them he used to jokingly exclaim 'oh no, the cat's scratching again!' Green's niece, Joan, remembers Hugh playing in the parlour to her and her boyfriend after they had attended church. May used to make tea and toast for them.

Green was part of a Bridge of Allan based group, who used to listen to and play music together. He gave violin recitals at various clubs and societies in the village. One of his relatives recalled one such event, when he played alongside a Mr Waller to accompany a play, performed by a local theatre group. Green also played at a great number of functions in St Saviour's church. In the 1950s the Stirling Circle included musical evenings in its winter programme, which Sydney L.K. Crookes ARCM usually organised. Crookes played the piano and was accompanied by Green on the violin. They usually played classical pieces. For instance, at a meeting held in December 1956 Hugh accompanied Crookes in performances of Beethoven's Sonata No.5 in F Major for piano and violin, in Tchaikovsky's Chant sans paroles and Crookes' own composition. The success of the duo came to an end when Crookes left for Yorkshire in the winter of 1957.

Green also used to play the violin to his friends, one of whom was William Steel. Green knew him around the time he was provost of Bridge of Allan (from 1959 until 1962). He used to have supper with him once a week at his house 3 Well Road and play the violin to him after they had finished their meal. William was a pianist so they sometimes played music together. William was also a keen photographer and took many pictures of Green playing the violin. William moved to Bridge of Allan in the late 1940s to retire. He had previously lived in Singapore, where he worked in banking. During the Second World War he ended up in a Japanese POW camp. In retrospect he said the experience was nothing compared to the trenches in France, which he had fought in during the First World War.

William was a founder of the Dr Welsh Educational and Historical Trust, an archive containing historical material pertaining to Bridge of Allan. The Trust was named after Dr William Halliday Welsh, who was a well-regarded GP in the village. Green

53. Hugh Green playing the violin, image provided by Ian Anderson.

was a friend of Dr Welsh and used to visit him every other Saturday to play the violin to him. Dr Welsh was a formidable character and lived life to the full. He had a distinguished academic career, fought in the war and was a keen sportsman, having played Rugby at national level. He was a bachelor and had a dog for company. Once when Green was playing Dr Welsh's dog started yowling. Hugh said he would have to stop playing if it was upsetting the dog. Dr Welsh explained to him that the dog was actually just expressing the fact that he was enjoying listening to the music.

HUGH GREEN'S DEATH

Hugh Green was sitting in his usual place at a service at St Saviour's when he was taken ill.

HE WAS RUSHED to Stirling Royal Infirmary, but died within a short space of time on 4 January 1973. He was eighty years old. In his will Hugh Green left £100 to St Saviour's Episcopal Church and the rest of his estate to Norman, his executor. Hugh Green had bought his right to be buried in lair no.25, section C13, Logie cemetery in advance as was customary. Robertson & Ramsay carried out the undertaking and Thomas Ross executed his memorial stone. A service was held at St Saviour's to commemorate him at 2pm on Monday 8 January. Later the same day he was buried at Logie cemetery and a meal was held in the Park Guest House in his honour.

HUGH GREEN'S FAMILY AND FRIENDS

Much of the information gathered in this publication has been kindly provided by Hugh Green's relatives and friends.

OFTEN THEY HAVE BROUGHT out his character by contrasting it to those of his siblings. According to one member of the family, Hugh was a father figure, who everybody went to for advice. The stories of his relatives and friends are inextricably intertwined with his. It is worth recounting them to further enlighten readers on the subject of Hugh Green's life.

Janet (b.1894), Hugh Green's Sister

Janet McLaren Arnott Green was born on 18 March 1894 at Kierfield, Bridge of Allan. Little is known of her life; she moved to Wales in the 1920s.

Willie (b.1896), Hugh Green's Brother

Peter William Green, known as Willie, was born on 30 March 1896 at Albert Place, Bridge of Allan. He was a 'tiny, wee guy', being only 5'1" tall, but was also 'a bit dumpy'. He was affectionately known as 'the wee one'. As a baby he was so small that his mother was able to put him in the bottom drawer of the gas range to keep him warm.

Willie served with the bantams during the Great War. A bantam is a small fighting cock, but the word bantam was used to refer to men, who did not meet the height required by regulations, but who were recruited in spite of this. Willie may have been a sharp shooter as he had had experience of shooting before he signed up. He had been a member of the rifle club in Bridge of Allan. They practiced target shooting with .22 Long Rifles. He returned from the war completely unscathed.

After the war Willie worked as a shoemaker in the village. Like Hugh Green he never married, but in many other ways he was quite a different character from his retiring brother. He was very lively, popular and sociable. He used to whistle as he walked around the village, wearing plus fours. He was very outgoing and was into everything. He was a member of the bowling club and was the local golf club champion. He died on 22 September 1964.

Davie (b.1897), Hugh Green's Brother

David Arnott Green was born on 19 October 1897 in Craig View Cottage, Fountain Road, Bridge of Allan. The Rector of St Saviour's church, William Edwin Hall, baptised him in December. Like his brother Willie, Davie also had been a member of the Bridge of Allan Rifle Club, fought in the Great War as a bantam and survived. Unlike Willie, he came back from the war a lot less healthy than when he signed up.

After the war Davie became a baker at Mathieson's, on the corner of New Street and Henderson Street. He met his wife Kate whilst on his bakery delivery round. She was housekeeper to a teacher at Greenloaning School. They had no children. David Green died on 25 June 1962.

Jack (b.1903), Hugh Green's Brother, and his Family

John Alexander Arnott Green, known as Jack, was born on 14 January 1903 at Allanview, Bridge of Allan. Jack worked at the textile bleaching, dyeing and printing factory in Ashfield, which was owned by the wealthy Pullar family. J. & J. Pullar and Company had bought the site and constructed the works in 1865. The Pullar's main textile factory was the Kierfield works in Bridge of Allan. Jack lived in one of the houses on Avenue Park provided by the Pullars for the workers they hired. The Pullars supplied the workers with various facilities, including a reading room. Jack was outgoing and mixed with everybody. In his spare time he enjoyed playing football and participating in running races.

Jack married Elizabeth Prentice, known as Lizzy, from Falkirk. Lizzy gave birth to a son, John, and a daughter, Jane, who was known as Jean (now Jean McLaren). John was a little handicapped and missed some school because of it. As a young boy John became good friends with Ella's son, Norman. Lizzy died when she was thirty-eight years old on 12 May 1940. Jack later married a lady called Agnes.

Jean grew up at Avenue Park and remembered crossing the Allan Water to go to school. She was only twelve when her mother died and used to feel a bit left

54. Ballroom, watercolour on paper, 590 x 690, collection of Jean McLaren.

out when Agnes and Jack had dinner together. Jean was very fond of her uncle James and his wife, Chrissie. She visited them often after her mother died.

Hugh Green sometimes looked after Jean and John. Hugh took Jean, John and Norman home with him after Sunday school. They had lunch with Hugh's mother and brother Willie. Hugh showed John, Jean and Norman his paintings and played the violin to amuse them. Jean later asked Hugh to be the godfather of her two children, Irene and Colin.

A member of the choir at St Saviour's, Jean saw a lot of Hugh Green. When she was a teenager she got a job at the Turnbull's bacon factory. After she moved to Crieff to work as a nurse she saw less of him. Jean said that Hugh was a lovely man and set a good example for her to follow. She now has a large collection of his paintings, including a large ballroom scene, an unusual subject matter for him (fig. 54).

May (b.1904), Hugh Green's Sister

Mary Jane Berry Arnott Green, known as May, was born on 2 October 1904 at Allanbank, Bridge of Allan. William Hall baptised her at St Saviour's in November. Like Hugh Green she was small, quiet and 'stick thin'. For a time, May was a civil servant and worked in the pension's office in Stirling. May was quite strict and thought it improper for you to have your hands in your pockets.

A German Jewish man called Alfred Samuel George Racher, known as George, fell in love with May. George lived at 7 Bower Street, Glasgow and used to visit May once a week. George wanted to marry May and proposed to her several times, but she never accepted. May died on 29 December 1968 without having married him. In her will she left £100 to him. He relinquished any claim to the money and gave his part to Norman. George gave the ring he had bought for May to Norman's wife, Elizabeth. Hugh Green thought a great deal of George. He specifically expressed his wish in his will that George be buried with him in his lair at Logie cemetery, Bridge of Allan.

Ella (b.1906), Hugh Green's Sister, and her Family

Helen Arnott Green, known as Ella, was born on 22 September 1906 in Allanbank. William Hall baptised her at St Saviour's in November. Like Hugh Green, Ella was also artistically talented: in her youth she worked as a carpet designer at the Templeton's factory in Glasgow. The intricacy of her designs evidences her remarkable skill (figs. 55 & 56). Ella's marriage to Robert Graham and their son Norman have already been mentioned. They lived together above Mathieson's the baker's. Robert earned money for the family as a policeman so that Ella was able to stop working to look after Norman. Robert had suffered from shrapnel wounds in the Great War, which affected his health, possibly leading to his early death. After that Ella took a job at the Dreadnought Hotel, Callander. During the day Norman's granny looked after him at Allanbank so that Ella could go to work.

After the Second World War Ella married Robert Brown Gordon, known as Rab. He had worked with the Stirlingshire Constabulary from 1934. A war hero, he resumed work with the police in December 1946. He quickly rose up through the ranks and became Commander of the Scottish Crime Squad in 1969. When Rab became commissioner of police in Gibraltar in 1974, he and Ella moved out there for a number of years, before retiring to Braco. Ella died in January 1993 whilst Rab died in January 2000.

Norman worked as an assistant to Hugh Green at his painting and decorating business from a young age and became very devoted to him. He painted the clock with him as a young boy. Norman was naturally talented at practical work or as one of his

55. Carpet design by Ella Green.

56. Carpet design by Ella Green.

friends put it 'he had clever hands'. He was ambidextrous and used to paint the lettering on the Turnbull's butchery distribution vans with both hands at the same time! He wrote signs as a hobby and did not just do it for work. Norman was also a skilled artist and painted pictures of the local area. Sometimes Hugh drew sketches, which Norman coloured and finished. Norman was interested in Scottish history. He used to restore antique objects, such as old lamps. He also worked at various historic sites, as a tour guide at Stirling Castle and as a boat man at the Lake of Menteith.

Norman married his wife Elizabeth in 1956. Hugh Green gave them a sideboard, table and chairs as wedding presents. Norman and Elizabeth had a daughter together, who they called Yvonne. Norman bought lots of Hugh's paintings from the yearly exhibitions at St Saviour's. When Norman and Elizabeth lived at 35 Cawder Road, Bridge of Allan it was impossible to see the walls for the pictures. Norman inherited Hugh's estate upon his death and gave away many of his paintings to his friends and relatives.

Elizabeth worked as the housekeeper for Eric Pullar and his family, who lived on Chalton Road, Bridge of Allan. Hugh Green was a good friend of Eric and used to enjoy visiting him. Like Hugh, Eric was a longstanding member of the vestry at St Saviour's. Sometime after Hugh had returned from Majorca in c.1956, Elizabeth staged an exhibition of work by local artists in the basement of the Pullar's house with the backing of Eric to raise funds for the church. Hugh showed his work at the exhibition and sold many paintings. Later in life Norman moved from Bridge of Allan to St Ninians; he died recently.

James (b.1909), Hugh Green's Brother, and his Family

James Robert Graham Green, known to some as Jimmy, was born on 10 January 1909 at Allanbank, Bridge of Allan. James married his wife Chrissie and in 1933 moved to a little house in Union Street. James and Chrissie's first child, Hugh, was born there in 1934. In 1935 the family moved to an upstairs flat in a building on Allanvale Road, which was located opposite the old rifle range. The building was on the east side of the road near to the junction of Allanvale Road with Queen's Lane. It has since been demolished. James and Chrissie's second child, Joan, was born there in 1936. Shortly afterwards James went away to fight in the Second World War. He returned unscathed. James and Chrissie's third child, Hamish, was born in 1942 shortly after his return. In 1947 the family moved to a council house, 24 Cornton Crescent. There James and Chrissie had two more children, Tommy (b.1947) and Norma (b.1954). Chrissie died when Norma was only three years old.

For many years James worked as an assistant to Hugh Green at his painting and decorating business. James used to paint houses with him in the summer. He also put up wallpaper and was extremely good at it. For about four or five weeks in the winter he could not carry out painting jobs because the paint was so cold it would not run smoothly. During these months he varnished coffins with Robertson & Ramsay. Hugh Green used to visit the family home every Sunday, and share walks along the river.

When Hugh Green retired around c.1960 Jimmy looked for work elsewhere. He got a job with the Cape Asbestos Company (now Cape plc.), producing fibreglass in their factory in Kerse Road. He hated the work because he used to get fibreglass splinters stuck in his hands. Sometime later James managed to get a job as a painter with the Kork-n-Seal factory, which suited him well. James used to paint all the machinery and the interiors of the houses, where the workers lived. After being made redundant he worked for the painters and decorators Mackenzie and Pole who were based in a building behind the flats on Union Street, opposite the masonic hall.

Like many of the tradesmen James was on the fire brigade. A photograph was taken of him standing on the fire engine (fig. 57). He kept the fire-engine in a shed in Queen's Lane. Six firemen could fit on the engine. One notable local fire occurred at the Kork-n-Seal. Hugh Green took many pictures of it showing the extent of the blaze. Colour slides of the photographs are now held in the Stirling Council Archives.

James' son, Hugh (b.1934) and his family

Hugh was born on 24 July 1934. James named Hugh after Hugh Green. Hugh used to walk to Allanbank to visit Hugh Green as a young boy. Sometimes Hugh Green used to take the boy on holiday with him and the two became extremely close. Hugh was even closer to Hugh Green than he was to his father. Hugh respected Hugh Green and looked up to him as a role model.

The two of them happened to look very similar and had similar characters. Hugh, like Hugh Green, grew up to be very reserved and gentlemanly. Hugh's son, David, said that when Hugh Green died, it was the only time he has ever seen his father looking really upset.

Hugh grew up whilst Britain was fighting the threat of Nazi invasion in the Second World War and experienced the wartime blackouts. He later undertook an apprenticeship at the Kork-n-Seal factory. He worked as an engineer there and kept their machinery in working order. Afterwards he joined the merchant navy and Hugh Green bought his uniform for him. He had to be invalided out after going deaf. Hugh Green painted some pictures for Hugh of tankers (fig. 58).

Hugh married his wife Maureen in 1958 and moved to a house on Dumyat Road, Causewayhead. Hugh Green gave them some pictures he had painted as wedding presents. Hugh and Maureen had a son, David (b.1965). Maureen also helped to bring up Norma after her mother died. She used to tell Norma what her mother had been like. Maureen loved bringing up children. For two years she looked after a young Arab girl and boy, whose family had moved to Bridge of Allan from Saudi Arabia.

Willie and Hugh Green used to visit Hugh, Maureen, David and Norma every Friday evening without fail. He brought his violin with him and played music to them. He also attempted to teach David to draw. He asked David to draw local scenes such as the Wallace Monument from memory. David said he would have been about five years old then. He said that despite Hugh Green's encouragement he never took up drawing. Hugh Green gave David lots of his sketches as examples. As a young boy David added his own creative flourishes to some of them!

57. James Green standing on the Bridge of Allan fire engine, image provided by Ian Anderson.

James' daughter Joan (b.1936)

Joan was born on 20 November 1936. Joan was a precocious child and could read at a very young age. She used to read the newspaper to an elderly neighbour. He told her that if she became the Dux of the school he would take her for a taxi ride around Bridge of Allan as a reward. Joan did indeed become Dux of Bridge of Allan Primary School. She later became a chemist and took a job in a laboratory in Deanston. Sometime later she worked as a phlebotomist at Stirling Hospital.

James' son Hamish (b.1942)

Hamish was born on 23 January 1942. He worked as a television and radio repair man with the music shop, John M. Hay, in Stirling. Hamish once repaired the TV of the famous solicitor, Joe Beltrami, who lived in Glasgow. He was surprised to find that he had a painting by Hugh Green hanging on his wall, which he had bought at a sale at St Saviour's.

James' son Tommy (b.1947)

Tommy was born on 18 February 1947. Jean was made his godmother and carried him to his baptism at St Saviour's. When Tommy was about twelve he asked Hugh Green to make a copy of the picture printed on the front of a Christmas card for him (fig. 59). The picture was 'The Carpenter of Nazareth' by the American artist, Dean Cornwell (1892-1960). Cornwell was a very successful commercial artist in the 1930s and 1940s. Tommy said he thought that Hugh Green would not have considered the

59. The Carpenter of Nazareth (after Dean Cornwell), body colour on paper, 1960, 490 x 620, collection of Tommy Green.

painting finished. In spite of this everybody in the family was enthused by it. Tommy was around twenty-five when Hugh Green died. By that time he had begun working for the civil service in Glasgow and had lost touch with Hugh Green.

James' daughter Norma (b.1954)

Norma was born on 19 December 1954. Hugh Green was very fond of her. He used to take her to St Saviour's with him on Sunday mornings. After the service they would return to Allanbank and have lunch together in the kitchen. Hugh Green used to play the violin to her. Sometimes they would go for walks in the Mine Wood and sit in the gardens at the bottom of Blairforkie Drive. Norma remembers taking it in turns with her siblings to do errands for Hugh and his relatives at Allanbank on Saturday mornings. Hugh gave them pocket money for the jobs they did. Norma received a half-crown, which 'seemed a fortune at the time!' Norma now lives outside Washington DC.

58. Harbour, watercolour on paper, 490 x 680, collection of Maureen Green.

CHRONOLOGY

1870	The Burgh of Bridge of Allan is formed.
1889	Hugh Green's parents, Hugh and Jane marry at Kilsyth in November.
1892	Hugh Green is born on 5 February in Alloa.
1900	Colonel W.E. Gordon is awarded the Victoria Cross. He is the only person from Bridge of Allan to have been given the honour.
1902	Soldiers return to Bridge of Allan from service during the Boer Wars.
1907	Hugh Green starts working with the painting and decorating partnership, P. & R. Rose, in their workshop in Queen's Lane.
1908-9	Airthrey Mill Road (now Blairforkie Drive), the first modern road, is laid.
1913	Hugh Green's father died in February.
1914	King George V, Queen Mary and Princess Mary visit Bridge of Allan.
	The Great War begins on 28 July. Willie and Davie Green fight in the bantams. Hugh Green serves in the Local Volunteer Force.
1915	Hugh Green becomes an 'organ blower' at St Saviour's Episcopal Church, Bridge of Allan.
	The Glasgow School of Art awards Hugh Green an 'Evening School Award for Excellent Work' in textile design for the year 1914-15.
1918	The Great War ends on 11 November.
	Hugh Green is appointed to the vestry at St Saviour's
1928	The first ever meeting of the Stirling Circle of the Arts and Crafts is held on 19 October.
	Hugh Green becomes a member of the committee of the Stirling Circle in November.
1930	The Spa is reopened thanks to funding from the Town Council.
1939	The Second World War breaks begins of the 1st of September. The Stirling Circle closes for its duration.

1943	Hugh Green's mother died in August.
	Margaret, Alice and Helen Rose retire from P. & R. Rose and Hugh Green takes over the business in his own name.
1945	The Second World War ends on 14 August.
	Sir D.Y. Cameron, first honorary president of the Stirling Circle dies.
1946	The Stirling Circle resumes its activities in March.
1948	Hugh Green is appointed treasurer of the Stirling Circle in April.
1953	Hugh Green retires from the vestry of St Saviour's.
	The Stirling Circle changes its name to the Stirling Art Club.
1955	Hugh Green becomes vice president of the art club in April.
1956	Hugh Green is elected president of the Stirling Circle in April.
	Hugh Green goes on holiday to Majorca.
1957	The old bridge in Bridge of Allan is demolished and the new bridge built.
	Hugh Green travels to Ibiza for a holiday.
1960	Hugh Green resigns as president of the Stirling Circle.
1962	Hugh Green is appointed honorary president of the Stirling Circle in April.
1967	Stirling University is founded on the Airthrey Estate.
1968	Hugh Green is appointed honorary president of the Stirling Circle in April.
1970	The centenary of the Burgh of Bridge of Allan is celebrated.
1971	Queen Elizabeth II visits Bridge of Allan.
1973	Hugh Green is taken ill during a service at St Saviour's church and dies on 4 January at Stirling Royal Infirmary.
1975	The Burgh is dissolved as the Central Regional Council is formed.

EXHIBITIONS

Stirling Circle of the Arts and Crafts Exhibitions: 1929-1971

Stirling Fine Art Association Exhibition: 1938

The Royal Glasgow Institute of the Fine Arts Exhibitions: 1944 & 1946

St Saviour's Church Exhibitions: from c.1970

REPRESENTED IN COLLECTIONS

The Stirling Smith Art Gallery & Museum
Private Collections in Scotland, England and the USA

CATALOGUE

Artworks by Hugh Green
Sizes in mm, h x w

Stirling from the Raploch, body colour on paper, 1972, 320 x 485, collection of the Stirling Smith.

The Wallace Monument, watercolour on paper, 300 x 375, collection of the Stirling Smith.

Stirling from the Forth, watercolour on paper, 305 x 410, collection of the Stirling Smith.

Allanbank, watercolour on paper, c.1960, 400 x 500, collection of the Stirling Smith.

Stirling Castle, watercolour on paper, 1962, 255 x 350, collection of the Stirling Smith.

Airthrey Paper Mill, body colour on paper, 320 x 485, collection of the Stirling Smith.

Airthrey Paper Mill, body colour on paper, 370 x 480, collection of the Stirling Smith.

The Old Bridge, watercolour on paper, 370 x 480, collection of the Stirling Smith.

Hillfoots Village, body colour on paper, 370 x 480, collection of the Stirling Smith.

Stirling Castle, body colour on paper, 1971, 360 x 460, collection of the Stirling Smith.

Highland Loch, watercolour on paper, 210 x 280, collection of the Stirling Smith.

The Mine Woods, body colour on paper, 1972, 245 x 345, collection of the Stirling Smith.

Fishing Boats, watercolour on paper, 1960, 381 x 508, collection of Sue Porter.

Fishing Boats, watercolour on paper, 1959, 381 x 660, collection of Sue Porter.

Lecropt Kirk, watercolour on paper, 1963, 417 x 498 (incl. frame), collection of Joan Kerr.

Old Stirling Bridge, watercolour on paper, 198 x 343, collection of Joan Kerr.

Fishing Village, body colour on board, c.1915, 250 x 350, collection of Hamish Green.

Blair Logie, watercolour on paper, c.1930s, 200 x 290, collection of Hamish Green.

Fishermen Ibiza, watercolour on paper, 1960, 520 x 720, collection of Hamish Green.

Stirling Castle, watercolour on paper, 245 x 345, collection of Sheila McGregor.

The Carpenter of Nazareth (after Dean Cornwell), body colour on paper, 1960, 490 x 620, collection of Tommy Green.

Winter Scene, body colour on board, 1948, 318 x 415, collection of Charles Allan.

The Old Salt Works, watercolour on paper, 210 x 290, collection of Charles Allan.

The Old Salt Works, watercolour on paper, 250 x 340, collection of Charles Allan.

Fruit Market, watercolour on paper, 1959, 360 x 495, collection of Maureen Green.

Fisherman, watercolour on paper, 1959, 355 x 495, collection of Maureen Green.

Harbour, watercolour on paper, 490 x 680, collection of Maureen Green.

The Inverallan Mill, watercolour on paper, collection of Norma Lunney.

The Allan Water, watercolour on paper, 260 x 350, collection of Ann Wallace.

The Fountain of Nineveh, watercolour on paper, 1960, 345 x 495, collection of Carole McKee.

Cottage, watercolour on paper, 120 x 175, collection of Carole McKee.

Small Sketchbook belonging to Hugh Green, 125 x 185, collection of Carole McKee.

Fishing Boats, watercolour on paper, 755 x 945 (incl. frame), collection of David Green.

Blair Logie, watercolour on board, 490 x 655 (incl. frame), collection of David Green.

Puerto Soller, watercolour on paper, 1957, 560 x 700, collection of George McArthur.

The Drip Bridge, pastel & body colour on paper, 426 x 578 (incl. frame), collection of Isabel Steel.

The Wallace Monument, watercolour on paper, 269 x 370 (incl. frame), collection of Isabel Steel.

The Inverallan Mill Wheel, watercolour on paper, 1966, 320 x 395 (incl. frame), collection of Isabel Steel.

Evening (Stirling Castle), body colour on paper, 220 x 474 (incl. frame), collection of Isabel Steel.

Clydesdales, watercolour on paper, 345 x 470, collection of Jean McLaren.

River Scene, body colour on paper, 250 x 345, collection of Jean McLaren.

Rural Scene, watercolour on paper, 240 x 330, collection of Jean McLaren.

Ella and Norman Green in the Highlands, watercolour on paper, 1947, 480 x 325, collection of Jean McLaren.

Stirling from a Distance, 470 x 640, collection of Jean McLaren.

The Allan Water, watercolour on paper, 300 x 415, collection of Jeanette Allan.

The Mine Woods, body colour on paper, 1972, 300 x 400, collection of Jeanette Allan.

The Old Airthrey Paper Mill, oil on canvas, 1912, 280 x 415, collection of Yvonne Syme.

Paper Mill Cottages, pastel and body colour on canvas, 1934, 400 x 500, collection of Yvonne Syme.

The Weir on The Allan Water, watercolour on paper, 1965, 250 x 355, collection of Yvonne Syme.

Allanbank, body colour on paper, 195 x 260, collection of Yvonne Syme.

Allanbank, body colour on paper, 370 x 505, collection of Yvonne Syme.

Study of a Tree, watercolour on paper, 1959, 370 x 505, collection of Yvonne Syme.

Ship Building, watercolour on paper, 1959, 370 x 505, collection of Yvonne Syme.

Gateway, Ibiza, watercolour on paper, 1960, 245 x 345, collection of Yvonne Syme.

Stirling Castle, body colour on board, 1971, 570 x 830, collection of Yvonne Syme.

Stirling Castle from Raploch, watercolour on paper, 1967, 370 x 505, collection of Yvonne Syme.

The Fountain of Nineveh, watercolour on paper, 330 x 455, collection of Yvonne Syme.

Crail, body colour on paper, 370 x 505, collection of Yvonne Syme.

Fruit Market, watercolour on paper, 1960, 370 x 505, collection of Yvonne Syme.

Henderson Street, body colour on paper, 1971, 380 x 500, collection of Yvonne Syme.

Figure Study, graphite on paper, 380 x 560, collection of Yvonne Syme.

Figure Study, graphite on paper, 380 x 560, collection of Yvonne Syme.

Geometric Pattern, body colour on paper, 560 x 2230, collection of Yvonne Syme.

Floral Pattern, body colour on paper, 780 x 780, collection of Yvonne Syme.

Floral Design for Print, body colour on paper, 270 x 390, collection of Yvonne Syme.

Floral Design for Print, body colour on paper, 270 x 360, collection of Yvonne Syme.

Floral Design for Print, body colour on paper, 310 x 410, collection of Yvonne Syme.

Hunting Scene, body colour on paper, 590 x 1940, collection of Yvonne Syme.

Lesley Pullar, Elizabeth Graham and Yvonne Graham, watercolour on paper, 1960, 360 x 510, collection of Yvonne Syme.

Portrait, watercolour on paper, 190 x 270, collection of Yvonne Syme.

Floor Cloth Design, body colour on paper, 205 x 285, collection of Yvonne Syme.

Field of Flowers, watercolour on paper, 370 x 495, collection of Yvonne Syme.

Assorted sketchbooks and painting equipment, collection of Yvonne Syme.

Fishing Boat, watercolour on paper, 375 x 500, collection of Molly Orchard.

Lecropt Kirk, watercolour on paper, 1969, 245 x 345, collection of Molly Orchard.

The Old Toll House, watercolour on board, 1965, 380 x 660, collection of Dr Welsh Educational and Historical Trust.

BIBLIOGRAPHY

Books & Articles

Aitken, Peter, Cameron Cunningham and Bob McCutcheon. *Notes for a New History of Stirling: The Homesteads Stirling's Garden Suburb*. Stirling: n.p., 1984.

Allan, J. Malcolm. *Bridge of Allan in Old Postcards: a story in pictures 1895-1945*. Stirling: Stirling Council Library Services, 1996.

Allan, J. Malcolm. *Bridge of Allan in Old Photographs*. Stirling: Stirling District Libraries, 1989.

Allan, J. Malcolm. *St Saviours at 150*. Bridge of Allan: The Vestry of St Saviour's Church, 2006.

Baile de Laperriere, Charles, ed. *The Royal Scottish Academy Exhibitors 1826-1990: Volume 2 E-K*. Calne: Hilmarton Manor Press, 1991.

Ball, F.C. *One of the Damned: The Life and Times of Robert Tressell, author of The Ragged Trousered Philanthropists*. London: Lawrence and Wishart, 1979.

Bilcliffe, Roger. *The Royal Glasgow Institute of the Fine Arts 1861-1989: Volume 2: E-K*. Glasgow: The Woodend Press, 1991.

Bilcliffe, Roger. *The Glasgow Boys*. London: Frances Lincoln Ltd, 2008.

Billcliffe, Roger. *Mackintosh Textile Designs*. London: John Murray Publishers Ltd, 1982.

Bilcliffe, Roger. *Charles Rennie Mackintosh: The Complete Furniture, Furniture Drawings and Interior Designs*. Guildford: Lutterworth Press, 1979.

Billcliffe, Roger. *Architectural Sketches and Flower Drawings by Charles Rennie Mackintosh*. London: Academy Editions, 1977.

Burkhauser, Jude, ed. *Glasgow Girls: Women in Art and Design 1880-1920*. 2nd ed. Edinburgh: Canongate Books Ltd, 1993.

Crawford, Alan. *Charles Rennie Mackintosh*. London: Thames and Hudson, 1995.

Cruickshank, Graeme. *A Visit to Dunmore Pottery*. Stirling: n.p., 2002.

Cumming, Elizabeth. Hand, Heart and Soul: The Arts and Crafts Movement in Scotland. Edinburgh: Birlinn Ltd, 2006.

Dixon, George. "The Founding Decade of Modern Bridge of Allan, 1836-45" *Forth Naturalist and Historian* 27, (2004): 101-109.

Eadie, William. *Movements of Modernity: The Case of Glasgow and Art Nouveau*. London: Routledge, 1990.

Green, Hugh. "Hugh Green" *St Saviour's Episcopal Church Newsletter* (1973).

Harding, Albert W. *Pullars of Perth*. Perth: Perth and Kinross District Libraries, 1991.

Hendrie, William F. *Old Bridge of Allan and Blairlogie*. Catrine: Stenlake Publishing Ltd, 2007.

Howarth, Thomas. *Charles Rennie Mackintosh and the Modern Movement*. London: Routledge and Kegan Paul Ltd, 1952.

Larner, Gerald and Celia Larner. *The Glasgow Style*. Edinburgh: Paul Harris Publishing, 1979.

Lillie Art Gallery Milngavie. *Allander Pottery (1904-1908)* exh. cat., text by Allan, Jessie and Hugh Allan. Milngavie, 2008.

Maclean, Ella. *Bridge of Allan: the rise of a village*. Alloa: Alloa Printing and Publishing Co. Ltd, 1970.

Macleod, Robert. *Charles Rennie Mackintosh*. Feltham, The Hamlyn Publishing Group Limited, 1968.

Ruskin, John. *The Stones of Venice: Volume II*. 2nd ed. London: Smith, Elder and Co., 1867.

Smith Institute. *Stirling Fine Art Association Exhibition 1938* exh. cat., text by J. McNaughton et al. Stirling, 1938.

Steuart, Katherine. *By Allan Water: The True Story of An Old House*. Edinburgh: Andrew Elliot, 1901.

Thompson, Paul. *The Work of William Morris*. 3rd ed. Oxford: Oxford University Press, 1991.

Archival Sources and Documents

Letter from Hugh Green. September 9, 1970. Coll. 1152. Dr Welsh Educational and Historical Trust. Bridge of Allan Community Library, Bridge of Allan.

Photographs by Hugh Green. 1980s. Coll. 187. Dr Welsh Educational and Historical Trust. Bridge of Allan Community Library, Bridge of Allan.

Photographs by Hugh Green. 1960s. Coll. 188. Dr Welsh Educational and Historical Trust. Stirling Council Archives. 5 Borrowmeadow Road, Stirling.

Stirling Art Club Minute Book 1928-1938. Stirling Art Club Archives. Victoria Square, Stirling.

Stirling Art Club Minute Book 1938-1987. Stirling Art Club Archives. Victoria Place, Stirling.

Stirling Art Club Role of Members 1931-71. Stirling Art Club Archives. Victoria Place, Stirling.

Stirling Art Club Sales Record 1931-71. Stirling Art Club Archives. Victoria Place, Stirling.

Statutory Registers of births, marriages and deaths in Scotland.

Civil Registration of births, marriages and deaths in England and Wales.

INTERVIEWS

Ann & Sheila McGregor

Ann Wallace

Carole McKee

Charles Allan

David Green

Elizabeth Martin, Bill Martin & Yvonne Syme

George McArthur

Hamish & Hazel Green

Ian Anderson

Ian McLaren

Isabel Steel

Jean McLaren, Iain Milne & Irene Milne

Jeanette Allan

Joan Kerr

J. Malcolm Allan

Margaret Finlayson

Maureen Green

Molly Orchard

Norma Lunney

Sheena Rodden

Sue Porter

Tommy Green

Ursula Shone